# A Year to Remember
## For Those Whose ...
### 1934

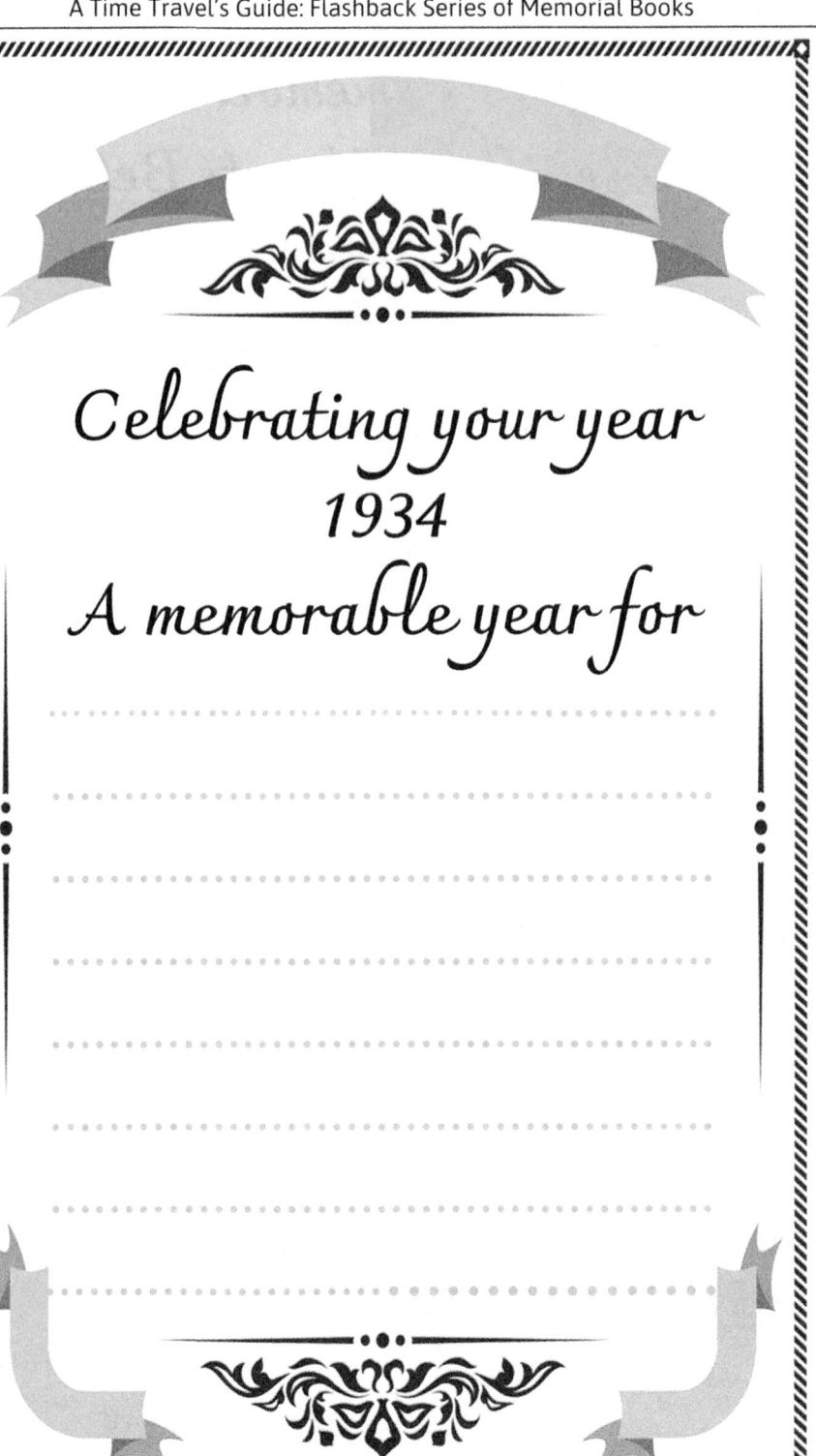

*Celebrating your year*
*1934*
*A memorable year for*

# *Content*

Introduction: A Glimpse into 1934..........5

**Chapter 1: Politics and Leading Events Around the World**
1.1 The Global Stage in 1934: Where Were You?..........6
1.2 Leaders and Statesmen: Movers and Shakers of '34..........12
Activity: Historical Trivia Quiz - Test Your Knowledge of '34..........18

**Chapter 2: The Iconic Movies and Awards**
2.1 Memorable Films of '34..........20
2.2 Prestigious Film Awards and Honors..........25
Activity: Movie Trivia Quiz - How Well Do You Know '34 Entertainment?..........27

**Chapter 3: Music: Top Songs and Albums**
3.1 Chart-Toppers..........29
3.2 Popular Singer and Bands..........35
Activity: Music Lyrics Challenge - Guess the Song Lyrics from '34..........39

**Chapter 4: Sports in 1934: A Journey Through the World of Athletics**
Achievements and Memorable Victories..........40
Activity: Search puzzle related to Sport winners in 1934..........51

**Chapter 5: Pop Culture, Fashion, and Popular Leisure Activities**
5.1 Fashion Flashback: What the World Wore in '34..........52
5.2 Leisure activities..........59
Activity: Fashion Design Coloring Page - Create Your '34-Inspired Outfit..........61

## Chapter 6: Technological Advancements and Popular Cars
6.1 Innovations That Shaped the Future..........................................65
6.2 The Automobiles of '34..............................................................70
Activity: Test Your Knowledge of Technology in 1934................77

## Chapter 7: The Cost of Things
The Price Tag: Cost of Living in 1934............................................79
Activity: 1934 Shopping List Challenge........................................83

## Chapter 8: Notable Births in 1934
Notable individuals were born......................................................86
Activity: "Profiles in Achievement: The Noteworthy Births of 1934"............................................................................................98

Special gift for readers.................................................................100
Activity answers...........................................................................101

# Introduction

A Year to Remember - 1934

For Those Whose Hearts Belong to 1934

Dear esteemed readers tied to the year 1934 through your birth, significant milestones, or cherished memories, this book stands as an homage to your unique bond with that remarkable time.

Within the forthcoming pages, we extend an invitation to embark on an enthralling expedition back to 1934—a year steeped in profound historical import. For those with an intimate tie to this era, it houses a treasury of recollections, narratives, and moments that sculpted the world and touched your lives deeply.

In the fabric of this book, we've interlaced the essence of 1934, intertwining historical perspectives, personal anecdotes, and engaging activities, enabling you to revisit and honor the significance of this extraordinary year.

As you turn the pages and immerse yourself in the events and culture of 1934, we hope you'll find moments of nostalgia, inspiration, and the opportunity to rekindle cherished memories of this extraordinary year.

This book is dedicated to you, our readers, who share a unique bond with 1934. May it bring you joy, enlightenment, and a deeper connection to the rich tapestry of history that weaves through your lives.

With warm regards,
Edward Art Lab

# Chapter 1: Politics and Leading Events around the World

## 1.1 The Global Stage in 1934: Where Were You?

The political landscape of the world in 1934 was deeply affected by the aftermath of World War I. Several countries were grappling with economic hardships, social unrest, and the rise of political extremism.

**The Night of the Long Knives (Germany)**

The Night of the Long Knives, known as "Nacht der langen Messer" in German, occurred on June 30 to July 2, 1934. It was a series of extrajudicial executions and political purges orchestrated by Adolf Hitler and the Nazi regime in Germany. Adolf Hitler orchestrated a purge within the Nazi Party, eliminating potential threats to his power, particularly the Sturmabteilung (SA) and its leader, Ernst Röhm. This event solidified Hitler's control over the party and the German government.

## The First Ever general strike in the US

In the depth of the Great Depression, in 1934, there were general strikes in San Francisco, Minneapolis, and Toledo. Industrial unionism was proving its mettle, and unions used audacious tactics, including sit-down strikes and roving pickets. When bosses compelled local governments to launch crackdowns or even summon the National Guard, many workers, both employed and unemployed, came to the defense of strikers.

*The 1934 Minneapolis General Strike*

*San Francisco General Strike*

## U.S. Securities Exchange Act

On June 6, 1934, President Franklin D. Roosevelt signed the Securities Exchange Act, which created the SEC. This Act gave the SEC extensive power to regulate the securities industry, including the New York Stock Exchange. It also allowed them to bring civil charges against individuals and companies who violated securities laws.

## 6 February 1934 Crisis in France

Violent riots erupted in Paris, organized by right-wing groups and anti-parliamentary movements, leading to clashes with the police. This event reflected political tensions and dissatisfaction with the French government's handling of economic challenges.

## The Revolution of 1934 in Spain

The Revolution of 1934 in Spain was a significant period marked by a revolutionary strike movement that occurred in the context of the tumultuous political landscape during the Second Spanish Republic. The trigger for this upheaval was the conservative Spanish Confederation of the Autonomous Right (CEDA) entering the Spanish government. Taking place between October 5 and 19, 1934, this movement was characterized by widespread strikes and revolts, particularly prominent in Catalonia and Asturias.

## The Soviet Union's admission to the League of Nations

The League admitted the USSR as a member in September 1934. The League of Nations, established after World War I, aimed to promote international cooperation, prevent conflicts, and find peaceful resolutions to disputes among nations. The Soviet Union's entry into the League was seen as a step toward diplomatic engagement and participation in the global community.

## The murder of Sergei Kirov, Soviet Union

The murder of Sergei Kirov on December 1, 1934, set off a chain of events that culminated in the Great Terror of the 1930s. Kirov was a full member of the ruling Politburo, leader of the Leningrad party apparatus, and an influential member of the ruling elite.

## 1.2 Leaders and Statesmen: Movers and Shakers of '34

1934 featured notable statesmen, whose actions influenced the world's political landscape. These leaders made lasting contributions, shaping their nations' destinies during a crucial period.

**Franklin D. Roosevelt**

Franklin D. Roosevelt served as the President of the United States in 1934. Roosevelt's administration in 1934 continued to implement the New Deal, introducing programs aimed at economic recovery, financial reforms, and job creation. He signed legislation like the Securities Exchange Act, regulating the stock market and expanding the federal government's role in the economy.

## Ramsay MacDonald

As Prime Minister of the United Kingdom. MacDonald's government in 1934 grappled with economic challenges caused by the Great Depression, implementing measures to alleviate unemployment and economic hardship. The government introduced limited economic reforms, including public works programs, though the impact was constrained by fiscal constraints. Internal political tensions within the coalition government strained its ability to address the economic crisis effectively.

**Adolf Hitler**

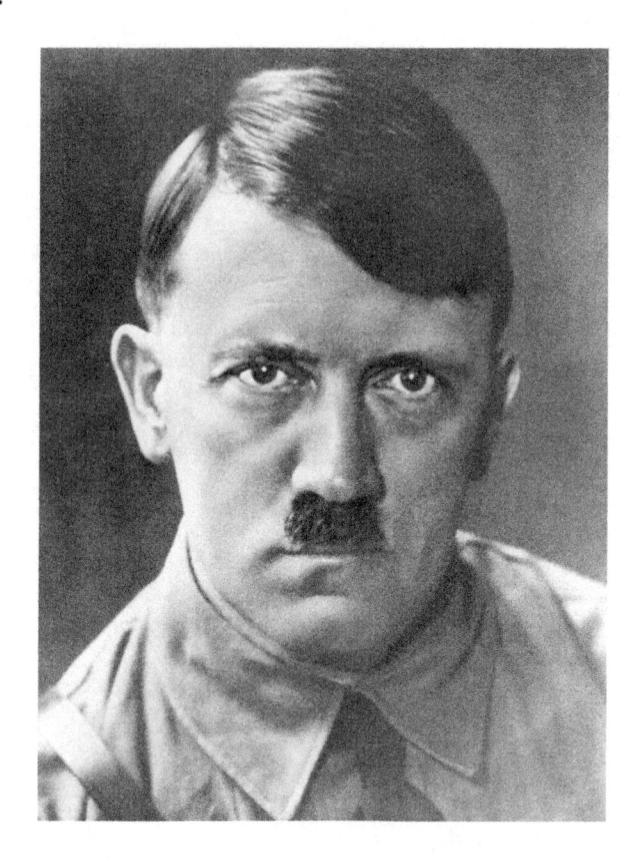

Adolf Hitler held the position of Chancellor in Germany during 1934, a year significant for the consolidation of his power and the further establishment of Nazi totalitarian rule. One of the pivotal events was the "Night of the Long Knives," where Hitler purged internal dissent within the Nazi Party, eliminating perceived threats and consolidating his authority. This ruthless action solidified his control and set the stage for absolute power. Furthermore, the death of President Hindenburg in August 1934 allowed Hitler to merge the roles of Chancellor and President, becoming the Führer of Germany. This consolidation marked a crucial step in cementing Nazi dominance and establishing Hitler's dictatorial control over the country.

## Joseph Stalin

Joseph Stalin was General Secretary of the Central Committee in the Soviet Union in 1934. Stalin's leadership continued the Soviet Union's path towards industrialization through collectivization and rapid industrial growth. Despite resistance and severe consequences, he consolidated power within the Communist Party, eliminating opposition.

## Joseph Lyons

Joseph Lyons was Prime Minister of Australia in 1934. Joseph Lyons continued his emphasis on economic recovery, implementing policies aimed at stabilizing the Australian economy amidst the Great Depression. He advocated for balanced budgets, introduced social welfare measures, and promoted national unity to address the economic challenges facing the country.

## Getúlio Vargas

Served as President of Brazil In 1934, Vargas solidified his authority through the establishment of the Estado Novo regime in Brazil. He centralized power, initiated labor reforms to bolster workers' rights, and laid the foundation for an authoritarian structure that would characterize his prolonged rule.

## Richard Bedford Bennett

As Prime Minister of Canada, Bennett's focus in 1934 was on implementing economic measures to counter the effects of the Great Depression. His government introduced relief programs and public works projects to stimulate the economy and create jobs, although these efforts faced criticism and limited success.

## Benito Mussolini

Benito Mussolini was Prime Minister of Italy in 1934. Continuing to reinforce fascist control, Mussolini strengthened his grip on power in Italy in 1934. He emphasized nationalist policies, suppressed dissent, and consolidated his authority through the Fascist Grand Council, further steering Italy towards totalitarian rule.

## Abelardo L. Rodríguez

Was President of Mexico until November 30 Rodríguez focused on economic reforms in Mexico, implementing public works projects and industrial development initiatives to combat the Great Depression's impact. His presidency laid the groundwork for Mexico's economic expansion and modernization.

# Activity:
# Historical Trivia Quiz
# Test Your Knowledge of 1934

Are you ready to challenge your knowledge of the significant events and key figures of 1934? Here's a historical trivia quiz to test your knowledge of the events and leaders in 1934:

1. Which event in Germany in 1934 involved a purge to eliminate internal opposition within the Nazi Party?
A) The Night of the Long Knives
B) The First Ever general strike in the US
C) U.S. Securities Exchange Act
D) February 1934 Crisis (France)

2. Who orchestrated the Night of the Long Knives in Germany in 1934?
A) Adolf Hitler
B) Joseph Stalin
C) Franklin D. Roosevelt
D) None of the above

3. What legislation was enacted in the United States in 1934 to regulate the stock market and securities industry?
A) The Night of the Long Knives
B) The First Ever general strike in the US
C) U.S. Securities Exchange Act
D) February 1934 Crisis (France)

4. What major political event occurred in Spain in 1934, involving a series of uprisings and insurrections?
A) The Night of the Long Knives
B) The First Ever general strike in the US
C) The Revolution of 1934 in Spain
D) U.S. Securities Exchange Act

5. Who was the Prime Minister of the United Kingdom in 1934?
A) Ramsay MacDonald
B) Joseph Stalin
C) Franklin D. Roosevelt
D) None of the above

6. Which leader was in power in the Soviet Union during the events of 1934?
A) Adolf Hitler
B) Joseph Stalin
C) Franklin D. Roosevelt
D) None of the above

7, Who was the President of the United States during the enactment of the U.S. Securities Exchange Act in 1934?
A) Adolf Hitler
B) Joseph Stalin
C) Franklin D. Roosevelt
D) None of the above

# Chapter 2: The Iconic Movies and Awards

The year 1934 marked a significant era in cinema, witnessing the release of several iconic movies that left an indelible mark on film history. Alongside these cinematic gems, prestigious awards ceremonies celebrated the outstanding contributions to the art of filmmaking. From the glitz and glamour of Hollywood to the innovation and storytelling prowess of directors, actors, and screenwriters, the year was a testament to the evolving landscape of the silver screen.

## 2.1 Memorable Films of '34

### It Happened One Night

Directed by Frank Capra and starring Clark Gable and Claudette Colbert, this romantic comedy became a critical and commercial success. It swept the 7 major Academy Awards, a feat only matched by two other films in Oscar history.

## The Thin Man

This detective comedy film directed by W.S. Van Dyke, starring William Powell and Myrna Loy, marked the beginning of the popular "Thin Man" series. It was well-received for its wit, sophistication, and the chemistry between the lead actors and this film received critical acclaim and left a lasting impact on cinema.

## Cleopatra

This historical epic, directed by Cecil B. DeMille and starring Claudette Colbert in the title role, was a lavish production that garnered attention for its grand scale and visual spectacle.

## The Man Who Knew Too Much

irected by Alfred Hitchcock, this thriller was among the notable works from the master of suspense during this era.

## The House of Rothschild

Directed by Alfred L. Werker, this historical drama depicted the rise of the Rothschild banking family. The film starred George Arliss and was praised for its performances and historical narrative.

## Of Human Bondage

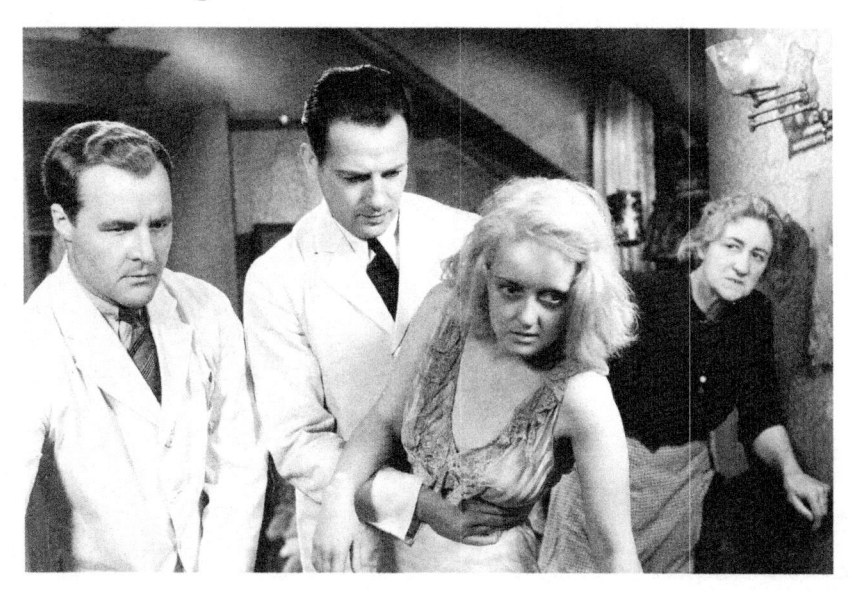

Directed by John Cromwell, this film adaptation of W. Somerset Maugham's novel starred Bette Davis and Leslie Howard. It was acclaimed for its performances and emotional depth.

## Twentieth Century

"Directed by Howard Hawks, this screwball comedy featured a fast-paced, witty screenplay and dynamic performances by its lead actors. Over the years, "Twentieth Century" has gained recognition as a classic comedy from the golden age of Hollywood cinema, appreciated for its comedic brilliance and the performances of its talented cast.

## The Black Cat

This horror film directed by Edgar G. Ulmer starred Boris Karloff and Bela Lugosi. Notably, it was one of the earliest movies to mix horror and psychological thriller elements.

## 2.2 Prestigious Film Awards and Honors

In 1934, several prestigious film awards were presented, honoring the outstanding achievements in the film industry during that year. Some of the notable awards included:

# Academy Awards (Oscars)

The 6th Academy Awards were held on March 16, 1934, to honor films released in 1933 .

**Outstanding Production:**
Cavalcade – Winfield Sheehan for Fox Film Corporation

**Best Director:**
Frank Lloyd – Cavalcade

**Best Actor:**
Charles Laughton for "The Private Life of Henry VIII"

**Best Actress:**
Katharine Hepburn for "Morning Glory"

## Academy Awards (Oscars)

**Best Supporting Actor:** Fredric March for "The Story of Louis Pasteur"
**Best Supporting Actress:** Jane Darwell for "The Informer"
**Best Original Story:** "One Way Passage" - Robert Lord
**Best Adaptation:** "Little Women" - Victor Heerman and Sarah Y. Mason
**Best Art Direction:** "Cavalcade" - William S. Darling
**Best Cinematography:** "A Farewell to Arms" - Charles Lang
**Best Sound Recording:** "The Song of Songs" - Paramount Studio Sound Department

## Activity: Movie Trivia Quiz
## How Well Do You Know '34 Entertainment?

**Introduction:** Let's test your knowledge of the iconic films and prestigious awards from the world of entertainment in 1934. Choose the correct answers (a, b, c, or d) for each question.

1. Who directed the film "It Happened One Night" released in 1934?

A) Howard Hawks

B) Frank Capra

C) Alfred Hitchcock

D) Ernst Lubitsch

2. Which famous couple starred in "The Thin Man" released in 1934?

A) Spencer Tracy and Katharine Hepburn

B) Fred Astaire and Ginger Rogers

C) William Powell and Myrna Loy

D) Clark Gable and Claudette Colbert

3. What was the setting for the majority of the film "Cleopatra" released in 1934?

A) Ancient Greece

B) Ancient Rome

C) Ancient Egypt

D) Babylonian Empire

4. Which film released in 1934 is based on a novel by W. Somerset Maugham?

A) "Of Human Bondage"

B) "Twentieth Century"

C) "The Black Cat"

D) "The Man Who Knew Too Much"

5. In "The House of Rothschild" released in 1934, the film tells the story of which family?

A) Vanderbilt

B) Rockefeller

C) Rothschild

D) Morgan

6. Who directed "Twentieth Century" released in 1934?

A) Frank Capra

B) Howard Hawks

C) Ernst Lubitsch

D) John Ford

7. Which horror film released in 1934 starred Boris Karloff and Bela Lugosi?

A) "The Invisible Man"

B) "The Mummy"

C) "The Black Cat"

D) "Dracula's Daughter"

# Chapter 3:
# Music: Top Songs and Albums

In 1934, the music scene was a lively tapestry of rhythm and melody, echoing the soul-stirring notes that defined an era. Explore the thriving musical diversity that marked the spirit of the times in 1934.

**Smoke Gets in Your Eyes**

Composed by Jerome Kern with lyrics by Otto Harbach for the musical "Roberta." This melancholic ballad captures the essence of lost love, evoking deep emotions through its haunting melody and poignant lyrics. The song's enduring appeal lies in its ability to convey a sense of longing and nostalgia, resonating with listeners across generations. Its emotive delivery has made it a timeless classic, with renditions by numerous artists cementing its place in the Great American Songbook. Paul Whiteman had the first hit recording of the song on the record charts in 1934.

## The Very Thought of You

Ray Noble's tender composition brings to life the essence of romance and yearning. Al Bowlly's rendition, among others, infuses the song with heartfelt sentiment, painting a vivid picture of affection and longing with every note, making it an enduring anthem of love.

## Love in Bloom

Bing Crosby's rendition of "Love in Bloom" echoes sentiments of blossoming love and tender devotion. The song's emotive lyrics, coupled with Crosby's velvety voice, created an enduring anthem for romance. Its timeless essence has secured its place as a quintessential love ballad, invoking feelings of warmth and affection in listeners worldwide.

## You Oughta Be in Pictures

Rudy Vallee's upbeat and charismatic delivery of "You Oughta Be in Pictures" encapsulates the lighthearted spirit of the era. The song's playful lyrics and catchy melody resonate with the dreamy aspirations of fame and stardom. Vallee's performance exudes charm, making it a delightful and enduring anthem that celebrates the allure of Hollywood dreams.

## Cocktails for Two

A playful and sophisticated tune, "Cocktails for Two" paints a musical scene of elegance and romance. It encapsulates the essence of a charming rendezvous, transporting listeners to an era of sophistication and amorous indulgence.

## Moon Glow

"Moon Glow" is a classic jazz standard that originated in 1934. Composed by Will Hudson, Eddie DeLange, and Irving Mills, this enchanting melody became popular during the Swing Era. The song's initial recording by Benny Goodman and his orchestra in 1934 catapulted it to fame.

## June in January

"June in January" is a timeless romantic song, popularized by Bing Crosby among other artists. Written by Ralph Rainger (music) and Leo Robin (lyrics), it debuted in the film "Here Is My Heart" in 1934, where Bing Crosby performed the song.

**The song's lyrical and melodic charm, combined with Crosby's velvety voice, has made it a beloved classic that continues to evoke feelings of romance and nostalgia.**

## Winter Wonderland

"Winter Wonderland" is a beloved holiday song composed by Felix Bernard (music) and Richard B. Smith (lyrics). Guy Lombardo's rendition of "Winter Wonderland" has become a classic, particularly during the holiday season. The song paints an enchanting picture of a wintry landscape and Lombardo's version stands out for its cozy and nostalgic feel, making it a perennial favorite for festive celebrations.

## 3.2 Popular Singer and Bands
### Rudy Vallee

- Rudy Vallee charmed audiences with his distinctive crooning style in songs like "The Very Thought of You," imprinting his romantic persona on these classics. Vallee's crooning approach and charismatic stage presence cemented his place as a prominent singing sensation during this period.

## Bing Crosby

Bing Crosby gained significant popularity with his rendition of "June in January" and "Love in Bloom" in 1934, captivating audiences with his velvety voice and emotionally resonant performances. His melodic tunes and charming persona solidified his position as one of the most beloved and influential singers of the era.

## Duke Ellington

Duke Ellington mesmerized listeners with tracks like "Cocktails For Two" and "Solitude" displaying his prowess as a composer and bandleader, while defining the era's jazz sound.

## Benny Goodman

In 1934, Goodman's contributions to the evolving jazz and swing styles were becoming increasingly apparent. His orchestra's performances hinted at the groundbreaking influence they would soon wield in shaping the Swing Era.

# Activity: Music Lyrics Challenge - Guess the Song Lyrics from '34

How well do you know the lyrics of the iconic songs from 1934? Test your knowledge with this Music Lyrics Challenge. Guess the Song's name from the Lyrics.

1. "The little ordinary things that everyone ought to do
I'm living in a kind of daydream"
..................................................

2. "In some secluded rendezvous
That overlooks the avenue"
..................................................

3. "Blue nights and you
Alone with me
My heart has never known such ecstasy"
..................................................

4. "Sleigh bells ring, are you listening?
In the lane, snow is glistening"
..................................................

5. "Oh what a hit you would be!
Your voice would thrill a nation,"
..................................................

# Chapter 4: Sports in 1934:
## A Journey Through the World of Athletics

## 4.1 Athletic Achievements and Memorable Victories

### 1. Football

Italy's victory in the 1934 World Cup on home soil was a monumental achievement, marking their inaugural triumph in this prestigious football tournament and sparking national celebrations across the country.

## The Football League

In the Football League of that year, Arsenal clinched the title with 59 points, securing the top position. Huddersfield followed closely behind with 56 points. Tottenham Hotspur finished third with 49 points, while Derby County and Manchester City shared the fourth and fifth positions with 45 points each, and Sunderland finished with 44 points.

## FA Cup Final

Manchester City emerged victorious in the FA Cup final, defeating Portsmouth with a score of 2-1. The match took place at the Empire Stadium, Wembley, London. The victory marked Manchester City's success in the prestigious tournament, adding another triumph to their football legacy.

## 2. Athletics

### Women's World Games

The Women's World Games showcased various sports and competitions exclusively for female athletes, held in London from August 9 to 11. This multi-sport event featured competitions in various disciplines, providing a platform for women athletes from around the world to showcase their skills and athleticism.

### European Championships Marathon

Arnas Toivonen of Finland emerged victorious in the European Championships Marathon held in Turin on September 9. Toivonen's remarkable performance saw him triumph in the marathon, completing the race in an impressive time of 2 hours, 52 minutes, and 29 seconds. His win marked a notable achievement in the realm of marathon running.

## 3. Baseball

### Major League Baseball All-Star Game

On July 10, the Polo Grounds in New York City hosted the second Major League Baseball All-Star Game. Historic Pitching Moment: Left-handed pitcher Carl Hubbell created history during the game by consecutively striking out legendary hitters Babe Ruth, Lou Gehrig, Jimmie Foxx, Al Simmons, and Joe Cronin. This incredible feat remains a memorable moment in baseball history.

### The 1934 World Series

The St. Louis Cardinals, led by brothers Dizzy Dean and Paul Dean, emerged victorious, winning the series 4-3 against the Detroit Tigers. The Cardinals, known as the "Gas House Gang," displayed formidable performance throughout the series.

## 4. Golf

In the world of golf during 1934, various prestigious tournaments witnessed remarkable victories

### Augusta National Invitational Tournament

Horton Smith clinched the Augusta National Invitational Tournament, an early version of what would later become The Masters, securing victory at Augusta National Golf Club.

### U.S. Open

Olin Dutra emerged triumphant at the U.S. Open, showcasing exceptional skill and technique to claim victory in this major championship.

### British Open

Henry Cotton secured the British Open title, displaying exceptional golfing prowess to win this esteemed championship.

## PGA Championship

Paul Runyan emerged victorious in the PGA Championship, displaying remarkable talent and resilience to capture this prestigious title.

## 5. Heavyweight boxing

Max Baer defeats Primo Carnera by an eleventh-round technical knockout at Long Island City to win the World Heavyweight Championship on 14 June.

## 6. Horse racing

Golden Miller's remarkable victories in both the Cheltenham Gold Cup and the Grand National in 1934 solidified the racehorse's legacy as one of the most illustrious and versatile horses in the history of British horse racing.

## 7. Basketball

In 1934, Argentina triumphed in the South American Basketball Championship held in Buenos Aires. The Argentine national basketball team secured victory in this prestigious tournament, showcasing their prowess and dominance in the sport within the South American region. This win marked a significant achievement for Argentine basketball

## 8. Ice hockey

### Stanley Cup

The Chicago Black Hawks emerged victorious in the Stanley Cup, defeating the Detroit Red Wings in a competitive series with a final tally of 3 games to 1.

### Ice Hockey World Championships

The 1934 Ice Hockey World Championships were held from February 3–11, 1934, at the Palazzo del Ghiaccio in Milan, Italy. Canada won its seventh world championship, defeating the United States in the final.

## 9. Tennis

**Australia:**
- **Men's Singles Championship:** Fred Perry from Great Britain emerged victorious, defeating Jack Crawford from Australia.
- **Women's Singles Championship:** Joan Hartigan Bathurst from Australia secured the title, defeating Margaret Molesworth.

**England (Wimbledon):**
- **Men's Singles Championship:** Fred Perry from Great Britain clinched victory, defeating Jack Crawford from Australia.
- **Women's Singles Championship:** Dorothy Round Little from Great Britain emerged victorious, triumphing over Helen Jacobs from the USA.

## 8. Tennis

**France:**
- **Men's Singles Championship:** Gottfried von Cramm from Germany won the championship, defeating Jack Crawford from Australia.
- **Women's Singles Championship:** Margaret Scriven Vivian from Great Britain emerged victorious, defeating Helen Jacobs from the USA.

**USA:**
- **Men's Singles Championship:** Fred Perry from Great Britain secured the title, defeating Wilmer Allison from the USA.
- **Women's Singles Championship:** Helen Jacobs from the USA claimed victory, defeating Sarah Palfrey Cooke from the USA.

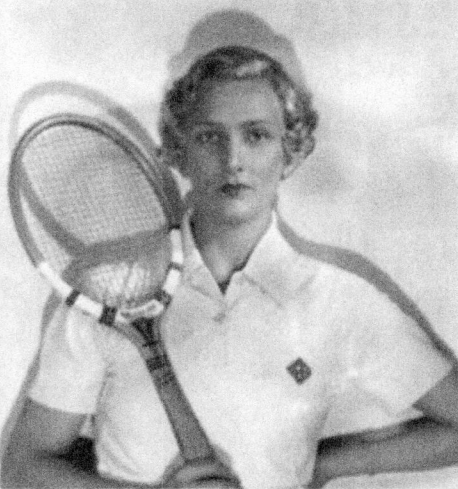

**Davis Cup:**
- In the 1934 International Lawn Tennis Challenge (Davis Cup), Great Britain emerged triumphant against the United States, securing victory with a score of 4-1 at Centre Court, Wimbledon, London, United Kingdom.

# Activity: Search puzzle related to Sport winners in 1934

Enjoy the multiple-choice quiz and see how well you remember the exciting sports history of 1934!

| M | A | N | C | H | E | S | T | E | R | C | I | T | Y |
|---|---|---|---|---|---|---|---|---|---|---|---|---|---|
| N | T | H | E | L | E | N | J | A | C | O | B | S | A |
| A | R | N | A | S | T | O | I | V | O | N | E | N | I |
| G | E | I | H | O | R | T | O | N | S | M | I | T | H |
| I | L | J | H | A | R | S | E | N | A | L | A | O | I |
| T | L | S | A | T | R | F | Y | I | L | R | T | O | E |
| R | I | P | E | F | O | O | T | A | T | S | H | F | O |
| A | M | O | P | A | U | L | R | U | N | Y | A | N | H |
| H | N | R | S | G | P | H | D | R | N | D | A | A | T |
| N | E | T | N | N | R | N | P | L | E | C | L | L | E |
| A | D | O | I | H | I | J | R | E | R | E | M | L | N |
| O | L | M | A | L | Y | A | O | L | N | N | T | T | I |
| J | O | P | O | F | R | E | D | P | E | R | R | Y | E |
| O | G | H | C | A | R | L | H | U | B | B | E | L | L |

SPORT     FRED PERRY     JOAN HARTIGAN
ARNAS TOIVONEN     MANCHESTER CITY     PAUL RUNYAN
GOLDEN MILLER     HORTON SMITH     HELEN JACOBS
OLIN DUTRA     ARSENAL     CARL HUBBELL

# Chapter 5: Pop Culture, Fashion, and Popular Leisure Activities

## 5.1 Fashion Flashback: What the World Wore in '34

Fashion in 1934 was influenced by the ongoing Great Depression, which affected the styles and materials used in clothing. Here's an overview of the fashion trends during that time:

**Women's fashion:**

**Elegant dress**

Fashion in 1934 reflected elegance and sophistication. Women's dresses often showcased sleek silhouettes and refined details. Hemlines generally fell below the knee, emphasizing a modest yet stylish look. Fabrics like satin, crepe, and velvet were popular choices, offering luxurious textures and sheen.

## Suits

In 1934, women's suits echoed a sense of sophistication and empowerment. They often comprised tailored jackets showcasing a balance between elegance and functionality. Fabrics ranged from tweed to wool, offering durability while exuding refinement. Jackets were tailored with defined shoulders and structured silhouettes, often featuring notched lapels or decorative buttons. Skirts maintained a modest length, emphasizing a professional and polished appearance.

The synthetic silk is ribbed like bengaline, its sole ornamentation being the clever white lace collar appliqued to it and brought across one side in a sweep. Details such as lace collars, ruffles, and intricate appliqués adorned many dresses, adding a touch of femininity and intricate craftsmanship to the overall look. The fashion of this era exuded a sense of timeless charm and grace.

Fashion for women celebrated well-defined waistlines, boasting dresses and suits tailored to accentuate the coveted hourglass figure. This shift away from the looser wartime styles marked a glamorous return to feminine silhouettes and allure.

## Hairstyle

In 1934, women's hairstyles exuded elegance and sophistication. Shorter haircuts, like the bob, remained popular, often styled with soft curls or waves to add volume and glamour.

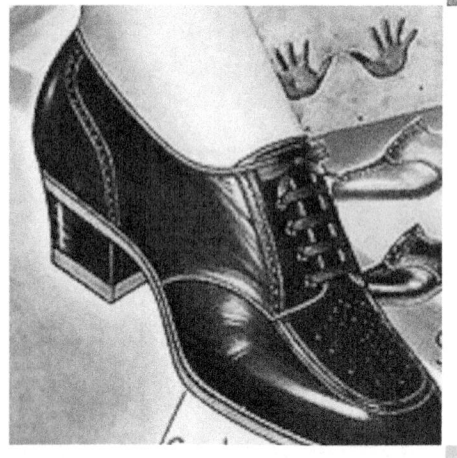

In 1934, women's shoes embodied classic elegance. The prevailing styles included Mary Jane shoes with low heels, offering both comfort and charm

## Cloche hat

Cloche hats, which maintained their popularity at that time, featured close-fitting designs that elegantly framed the face, often embellished with bows, feathers, or intricate detailing.

## Men's fashion

### Suits

Suits were a staple, typically featuring wide-shouldered jackets with structured silhouettes and high waists. The double-breasted suit was particularly popular, exuding a sense of sophistication and elegance. Trousers were tailored with a straight leg and often featured pleats, maintaining a classic yet comfortable style.

## Fedora hats

In 1934, men's fashion was indeed embracing fedora hats as a popular accessory. The fedora, characterized by its wide brim and pinched front, was a staple for men's fashion during that era. It was a versatile accessory that could be worn with various outfits, from formal suits to more casual attire, adding a touch of sophistication and style to a man's look.

## Lace up Oxfords

These were a staple in men's fashion. Oxfords were lace-up shoes with a closed lacing system, characterized by their sleek and formal appearance. They were commonly worn with suits and more formal attire.

## 5.2. Leisure activities

Stamp collecting, model trains, and board games gained traction as enjoyable leisure activities for many. These hobbies provided a means of relaxation, creativity, and social engagement for individuals during the era, offering a break from the challenges of daily life.

Vintage 1934 Champion Road Race Board Game

# Activity:
## Fashion Design Coloring Page - Create Your '34-Inspired Outfit

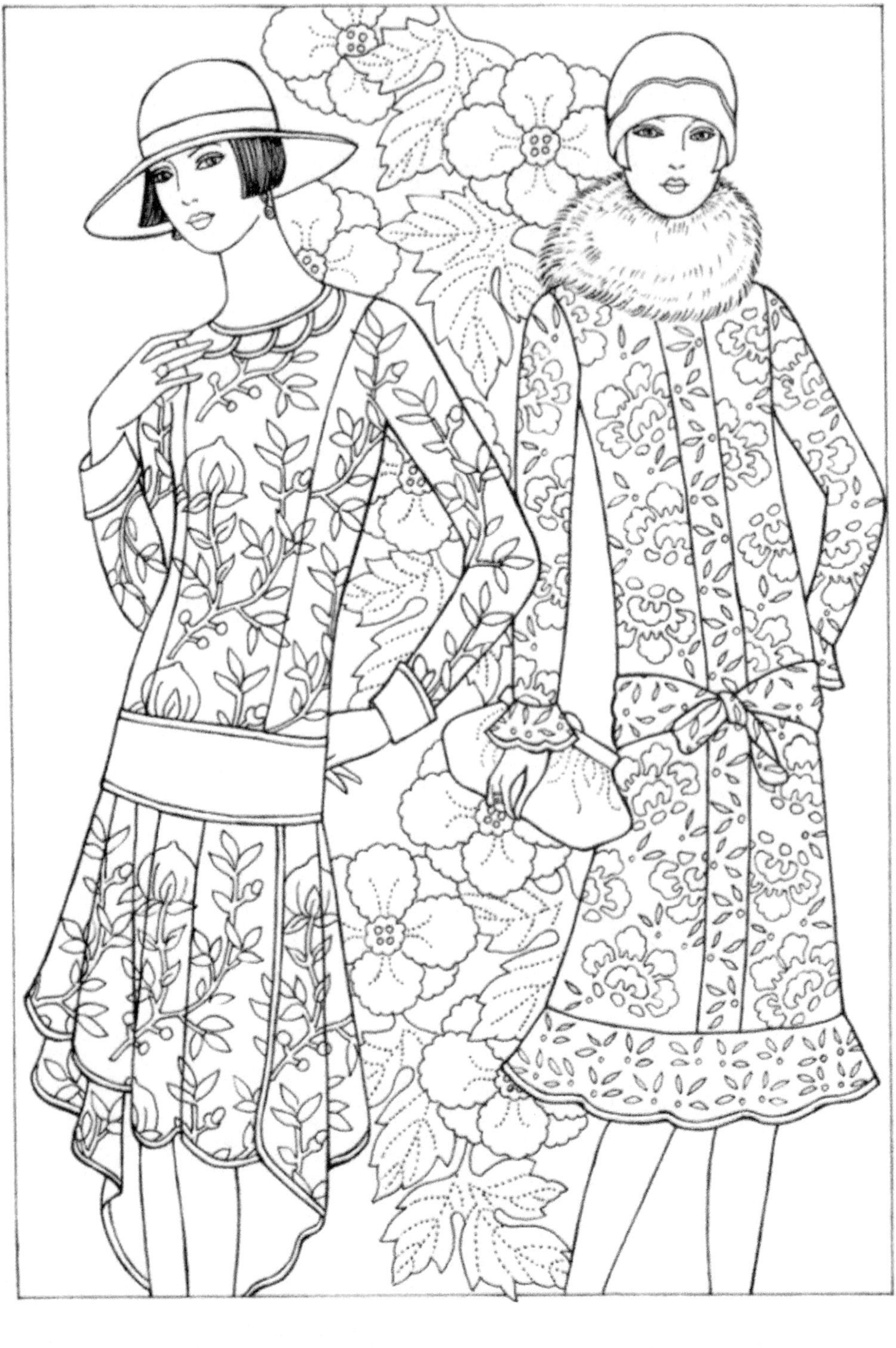

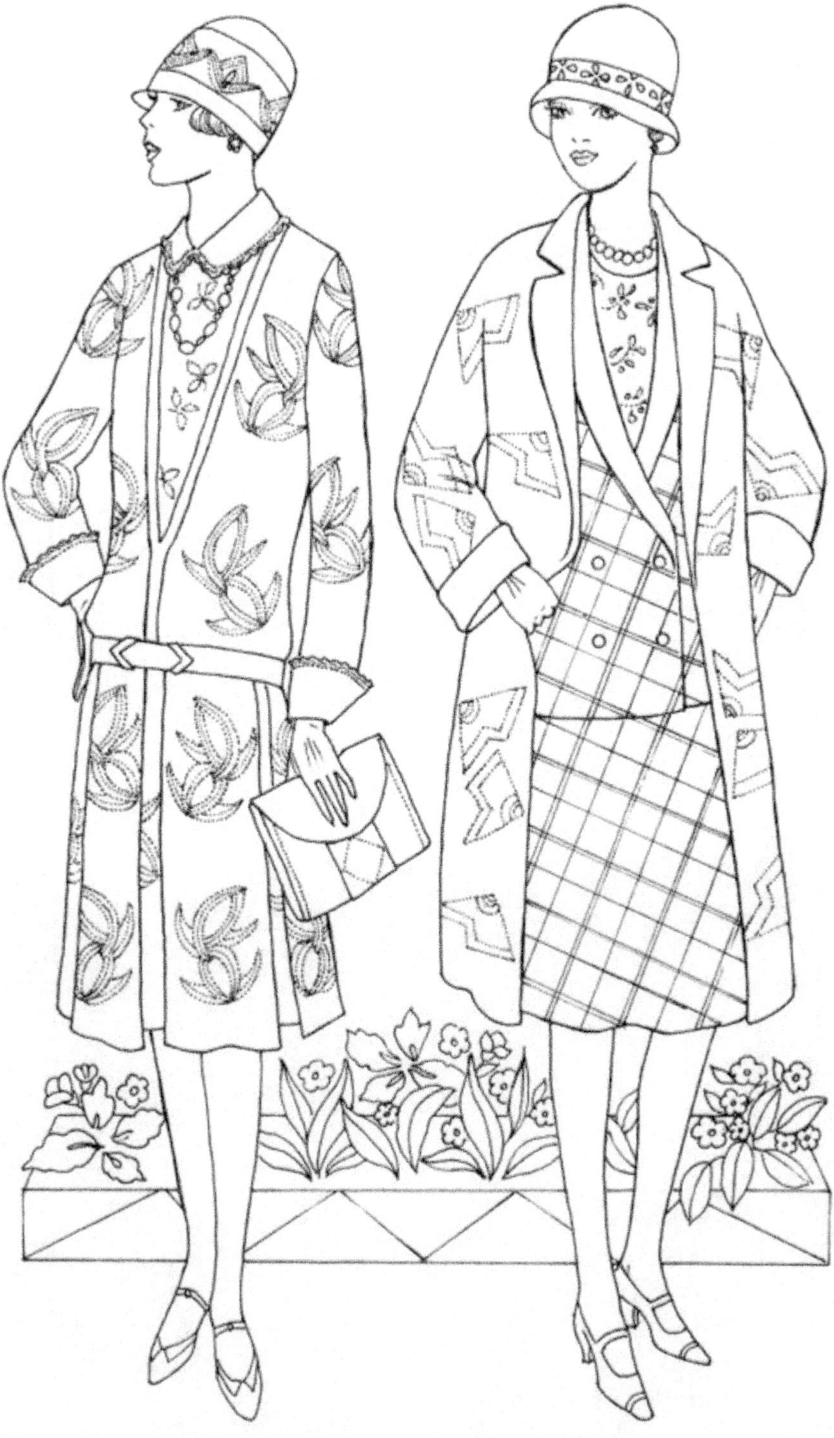

# Share your 1934 photos,
# Don't forget to show off your fabulous '34 fashion

# Chapter 6: Technological Advancements and Popular Cars

## 6.1 Innovations That Shaped the Future

The year 1934 witnessed groundbreaking technological advancements that laid the foundation for the modern era, ranging from innovations in computing to transformative developments in health and entertainment.

### Sikorsky S-42's Maiden Flight

In 1934, the maiden flight of the Sikorsky S-42 amphibious flying boat marked a monumental stride in aviation history. Designed by Igor Sikorsky, this aircraft symbolized the realization of transoceanic air travel dreams. The S-42's successful flight not only pioneered long-distance flights but also showcased the potential for extended-range aviation, facilitating intercontinental travel and transforming global transportation.

## Land Speed Record with The Flying Scotsman

Amidst the technological landscape of 1934, the legendary steam locomotive, The Flying Scotsman, etched its name into history. It achieved a monumental feat by officially clocking speeds of 100 mph, breaking new ground in railway technology. This iconic locomotive's record-setting velocity demonstrated the capabilities of steam-powered trains, pushing the boundaries of speed and efficiency in rail transport.

## The Launch of Queen Mary

The illustrious launch of the Queen Mary in 1934 heralded a new chapter in maritime luxury and engineering. This majestic luxury liner, christened in Scotland, epitomized opulence and sophistication. Its maiden voyage exemplified unparalleled comfort, setting new standards in transatlantic travel and becoming an emblem of maritime ingenuity, captivating travelers with its lavish amenities and cutting-edge design.

## Catseyes England by Percy Shaw

Percy Shaw's inventive creation, Catseyes, illuminated roadways across England, revolutionizing nighttime driving. These reflective road markers significantly bolstered safety, guiding motorists and enhancing road visibility in low-light conditions.

## Trampoline George Nissen and Larry Griswold

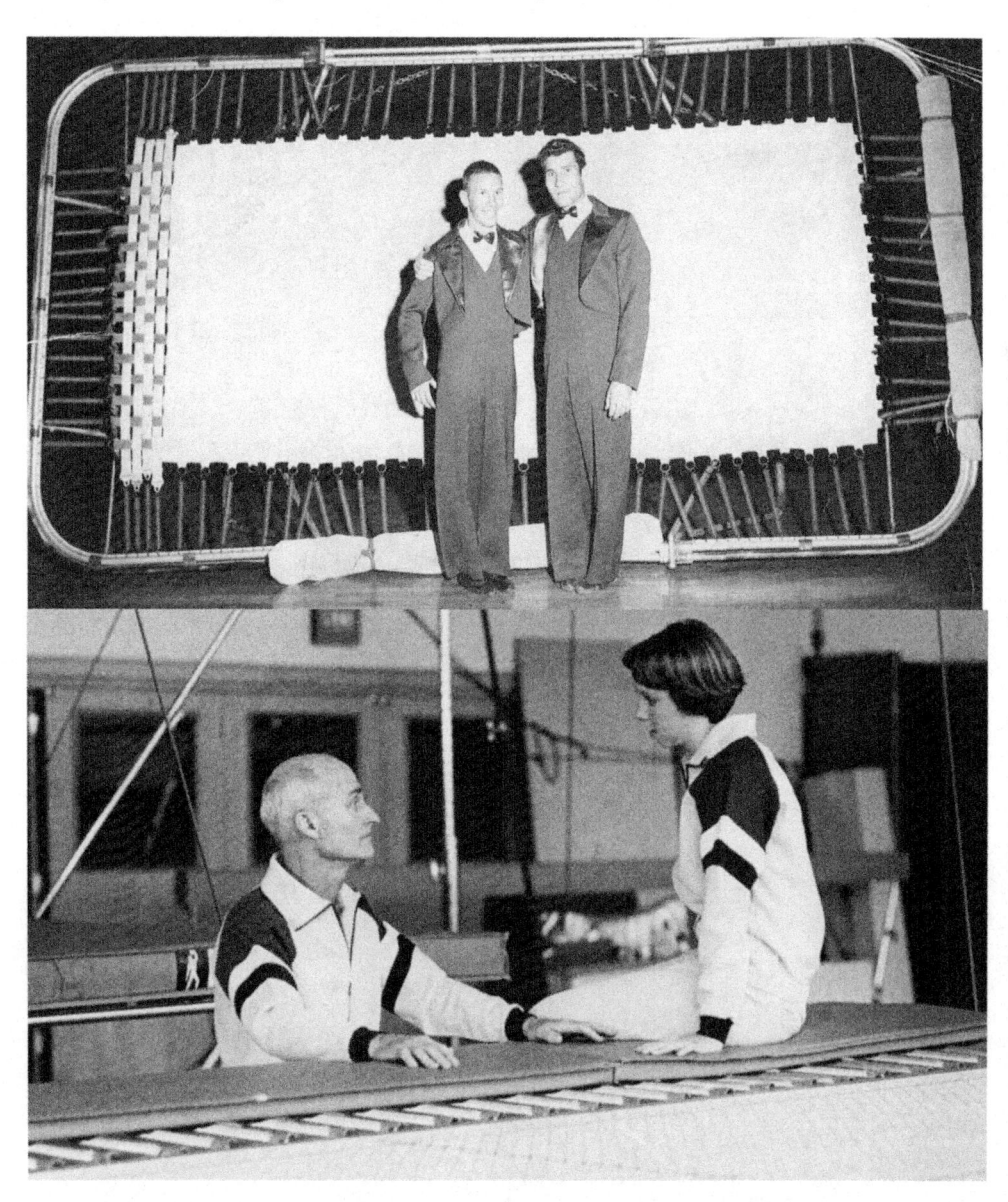

Meanwhile, the brainchild of George Nissen and Larry Griswold, the trampoline, transformed leisure activities. Its introduction offered not just amusement but also found utility in sports training and physical therapy, fostering a newfound realm of recreational athleticism.

## 6.2 The Automobiles of '34

In 1934, the automotive industry showcased several notable models and advancements that contributed to the evolution of automobiles.

### Chevrolet Master

Chevrolet Master was a versatile and affordable vehicle offering various body styles, catering to diverse consumer preferences.

## Chrysler Airflow

The Chrysler Airflow was a pioneering vehicle ahead of its time. Featuring a radical streamlined design, it prioritized aerodynamics for improved fuel efficiency and stability. Its innovative body construction and placement of the engine over the front axle enhanced performance, setting a benchmark for future car designs. The Airflow influenced the industry's approach to vehicle design and engineering.

## DeSoto Airflow

The DeSoto Airflow, derived from Chrysler's Airflow concept, aimed to revolutionize automotive design. With a similar streamlined form, it incorporated innovations like a fully integrated body and advanced engineering for its time.

## Ford Model C Ten

The Ford Model C Ten, part of Ford's European lineup, represented a compact and economical choice for consumers. It featured a modest four-cylinder engine and a simple yet functional design, catering to practicality and affordability. Emphasizing reliability and ease of maintenance, the Model C Ten aimed to meet the transportation needs of the era's budget-conscious buyers.

## Lanchester Light Six

The Lanchester Light Six epitomized British automotive elegance and engineering finesse. With its refined aesthetics and advanced technology, it catered to the luxury car segment. Boasting a six-cylinder engine and a sophisticated chassis, it offered a smooth and comfortable ride, appealing to buyers seeking prestige and craftsmanship in their automobile.

## Opel 2.0 Litre

Opel's 2.0 Litre model represented a blend of performance and practicality. Featuring a two-liter engine and a versatile range of body styles, it provided a balance between power and everyday usability. Its sturdy construction and functional design targeted a diverse consumer base, offering a reliable and adaptable vehicle suitable for various driving needs.

## Adler Trumpf Junior

The Adler Trumpf Junior was a compact and innovative vehicle that gained popularity for its engineering ingenuity. With a small yet potent engine and a lightweight structure, it combined efficiency with spirited performance. Its forward-thinking design and reliability made it an attractive choice for consumers seeking a nimble and economical vehicle during a period of economic challenges.

The automobiles of '34 reflected a blend of technological advancements, stylish designs, and attempts to meet consumer demands amidst economic constraints. These vehicles not only showcased innovation but also reflected the societal and artistic influences of the time, shaping the automotive landscape for years to come.

# Activity: Test Your Knowledge of Technology in 1934

"Welcome to the Milestone Fill-in activity! In this engaging challenge, you'll have the opportunity to fill in words related to Technological events.

1, _____ was the first real transoceanic flying boat and had its maiden flight in 1934.

2. The Flying Scotsman becomes the first steam locomotive to be officially recorded at _____ mph.

3. The Luxury Liner Queen Mary is launched in _____.

4. Catseyes were invented in _____ by _____ for lighting roads.

5. The trampoline was invented by _____ and _____.

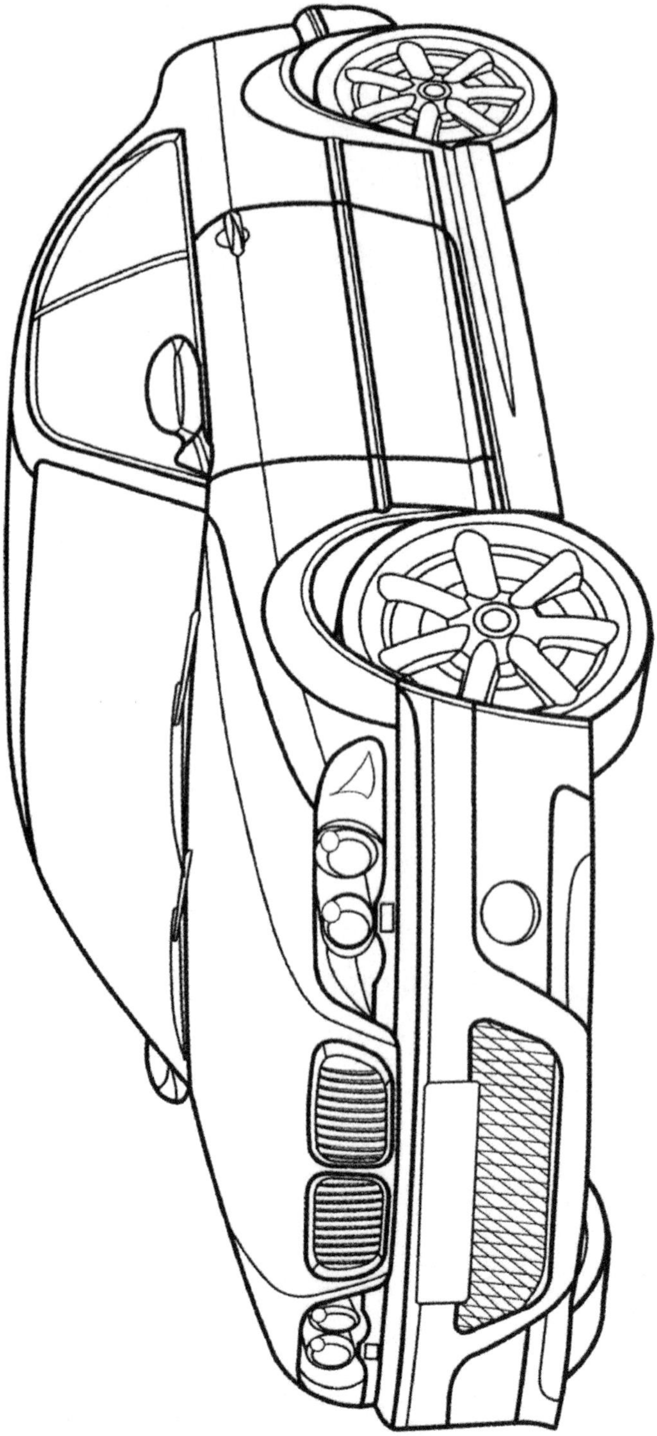

# Chapter 7: The Cost of Things

## 7.1 The Price Tag: Cost of Living in 1934

In 1934, the world grappled with the aftermath of the Great Depression, facing economic hardships and high unemployment rates. The cost of living was notably lower compared to modern standards, with food, housing, and transportation expenses reflecting a significantly more affordable era.

**Economic Indicators:**

- **Global Depression Impact**: The world was still reeling from the Great Depression, with many countries experiencing prolonged economic downturns and high unemployment rates.
- **High Unemployment**: Unemployment rates were severe, reaching alarming levels in various nations. In the United States, unemployment remained exceptionally high, hovering around 21.7% at the start of the year.
- **Slow Recovery**: Economies struggled to recover; while there were signs of improvement, growth rates remained modest compared to pre-Depression levels.

- Average Cost of new house $5,970.00

- Average wages per year $1,600.00
- Average Monthly Rent $20.00 per month

- Cost of a gallon of Gas 10 cents

- New Car $ 625.00

- A loaf of Bread 8 cents
- A LB of Hamburger Meat 12 cents
- White Potatoes 19 cents for 10LBs
- Heinz Beans 13 cents for 25oz can
- Spring Chickens 20 cents per pound
- Wieners 8 cents per pound
- Best Steak 22 cents per pound

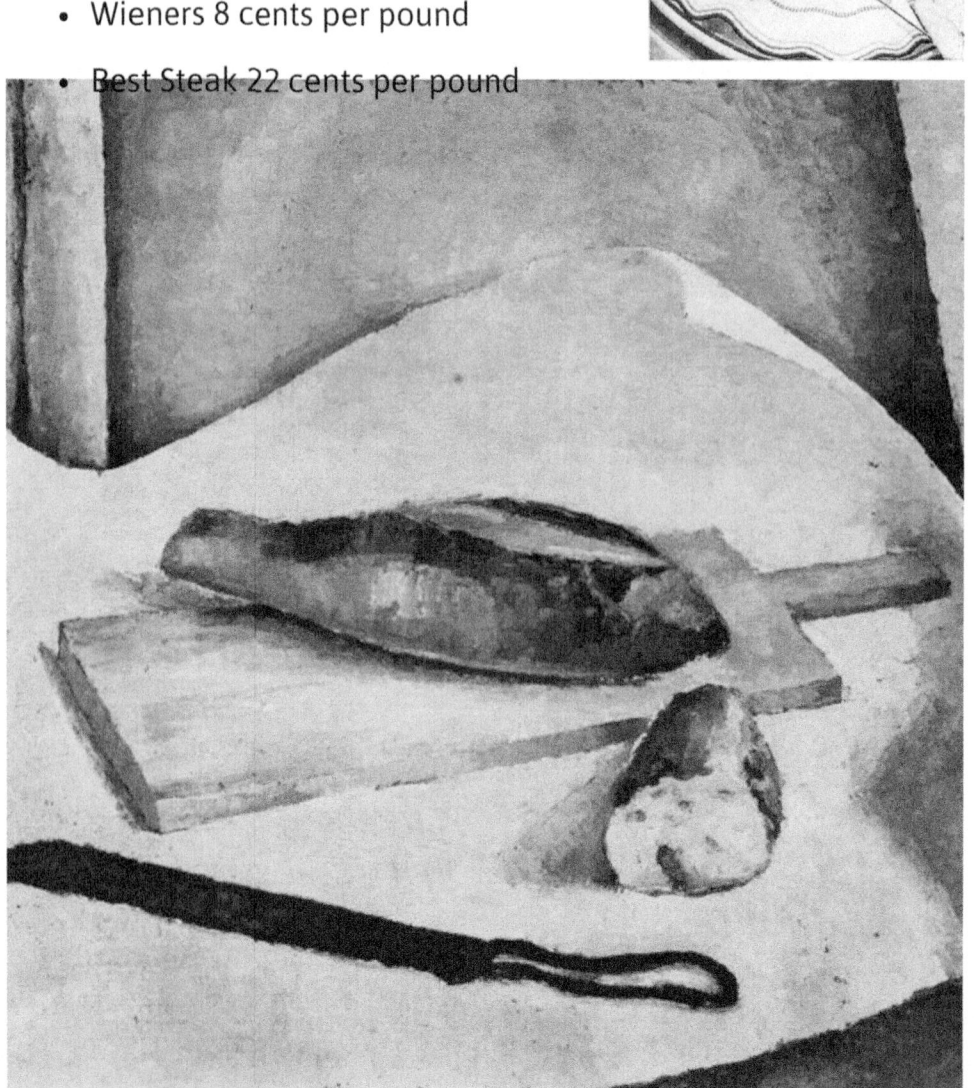

# Activity: 1934 Shopping List Challenge

Take this shopping journey through time, create a shopping list with these items, calculate the total cost, and consider how these prices compare to today's standards. Get ready for a fascinating glimpse into the cost of living in 1934!

**Shopping List:**

- Average Cost of new house $5,970.00
- Average wages per year $1,600.00
- Cost of a gallon of Gas 10 cents
- Average Cost New Car $625.00
- A loaf of Bread 8 cents
- A LB of Hamburger Meat 12 cents
- White Potatoes 19 cents for 10LBs
- Heinz Beans 13 cents for 25oz can
- Spring Chickens 20 cents per pound
- Wieners 8 cents per pound
- Best Steak 22 cents per pound

**Introduction:**

1. Create a shopping list that includes all the items from the list above.
2. Next to each item, write down its 1934 price.
3. Calculate the total cost of your shopping list in 1934 prices.
4. Now, let's bring this challenge to the present. Research and find the approximate prices of these same items today.
5. Create a second column on your list and write down the modern prices for each item.

6. Calculate the total cost of your shopping list using today's prices.

7. Compare the total costs in 1934 and today. Calculate the percentage increase in prices over the years.

8. Reflect on how the cost of living has changed between 1948 and today. What factors do you think contributed to these price differences?

## SHOPPING List 1934

| | Item | Price | # Units | Total Price |
|---|---|---|---|---|
| ☐ | | | | |
| ☐ | | | | |
| ☐ | | | | |
| ☐ | | | | |
| ☐ | | | | |
| ☐ | | | | |
| ☐ | | | | |
| ☐ | | | | |
| ☐ | | | | |
| ☐ | | | | |
| ☐ | | | | |
| ☐ | | | | |
| ☐ | | | | |
| ☐ | | | | |
| ☐ | | | | |
| ☐ | | | | |
| ☐ | | | | |
| ☐ | | | | |
| ☐ | | | | |
| | | | Total | |

# SHOPPING List Today

| | Item | Price | # Units | Total Price |
|---|------|-------|---------|-------------|
| ☐ | | | | |
| ☐ | | | | |
| ☐ | | | | |
| ☐ | | | | |
| ☐ | | | | |
| ☐ | | | | |
| ☐ | | | | |
| ☐ | | | | |
| ☐ | | | | |
| ☐ | | | | |
| ☐ | | | | |
| ☐ | | | | |
| ☐ | | | | |
| ☐ | | | | |
| ☐ | | | | |
| ☐ | | | | |
| ☐ | | | | |
| ☐ | | | | |
| ☐ | | | | |
| ☐ | | | | |
| | | | Total | |

This activity will give you a perspective on the value of money and how inflation has affected our purchasing power over time. Have fun with your 1934 Shopping List Challenge!

# Chapter 8: Notable Births in 1934

The year 1934 marked the birth of individuals who would go on to shape the cultural landscape across various domains, leaving an indelible mark on the world. Let's explore the careers and contributions of these notable figures.

**Brian Epstein (September 19th)**

Epstein, born in Liverpool, became the influential manager of The Beatles. Recognizing their potential, he guided them to global stardom, securing their record deal with EMI and transforming them into a cultural phenomenon. His business acumen and vision were instrumental in shaping the band's career trajectory and their impact on music history.

## Sophia Loren (September 20th)

Born in Rome, Sophia Loren emerged as one of Italy's most iconic and celebrated actresses. Her talent, beauty, and versatility on screen garnered critical acclaim, earning her numerous awards, including an Academy Award for Best Actress. Loren's performances in films like "Two Women" solidified her place as a cinematic legend, becoming a symbol of elegance and talent in the golden era of Hollywood.

## Yuri Gagarin (March 9th)

Gagarin, born in the Russian village of Klushino, made history as the first human in space aboard the Vostok 1 spacecraft in 1961. His pioneering orbital flight marked a monumental achievement in space exploration, cementing Soviet dominance in the space race and advancing our understanding of manned space travel.

## Hank Aaron (February 5th)

Henry Louis Aaron, born in Mobile, Alabama, rose to prominence as a baseball legend. His illustrious career in Major League Baseball saw him break records, including Babe Ruth's home run record, eventually culminating in 755 career home runs. Aaron's excellence on the field and enduring impact solidified his status as one of baseball's greatest players.

## Giorgio Armani (July 11th)

Armani, born in Piacenza, Italy, revolutionized the fashion industry with his sophisticated and minimalist designs. He reshaped men's and women's fashion, introducing elegant and tailored clothing that defined a new standard of luxury. Armani's influence extended globally, establishing him as an iconic figure in haute couture.

## Tom Baker (January 20th)

Tom Baker gained widespread recognition as the fourth actor to portray the Doctor in the iconic British television series "Doctor Who." His portrayal from 1974 to 1981 became iconic, embodying the eccentric and enigmatic character with a unique charm, earning a devoted fanbase and leaving an indelible mark on the show's legacy.

## Brigitte Bardot (September 28th)

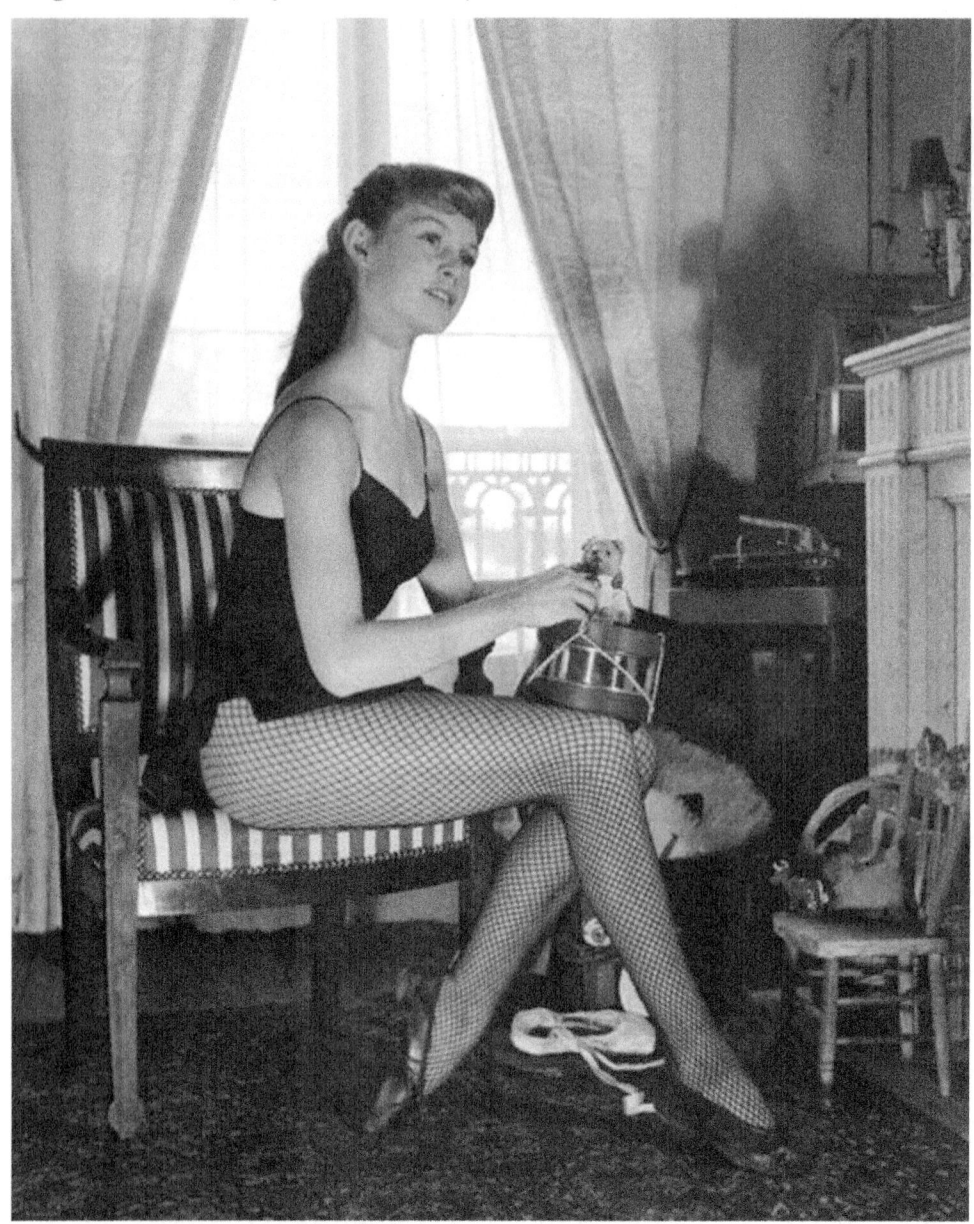

Bardot, born in Paris, emerged as an international symbol of beauty, style, and sexuality. Her acting career propelled her to stardom, and she became an iconic figure of the 1950s and 1960s cinema. Bardot's impact extended beyond film, influencing fashion, culture, and societal norms of feminine expression.

## Pat Boone (June 1st)

Pat Boone emerged as a prominent singer, actor, and TV personality. His smooth voice and versatility across various musical genres, including pop, gospel, and country, earned him numerous hits and a significant presence in the music industry. Boone's career spanned decades, leaving a lasting impact on American entertainment.

**Barry Humphries (February 17th**

Barry Humphries was born in Melbourne, Australia, Barry Humphries is a multifaceted entertainer known for his satirical comedy and character creation. He is notably recognized for his alter ego, Dame Edna Everage, a beloved comedic character known for wit, social commentary, and cultural satire. Humphries' impact extended across comedy, theater, and television, showcasing his creative brilliance and enduring influence.

## Roy Kinnear (January 8th)

Roy Kinnear was a versatile British actor known for his comedic talent and distinctive presence on screen. He appeared in numerous films, stage productions, and television shows, showcasing his versatility in both comedic and dramatic roles. Kinnear's notable contributions include appearances in movies like "Willy Wonka & the Chocolate Factory," "The Three Musketeers," and "Help!"

## Charles Manson (November 12th)

Charles Manson gained infamy as a cult leader responsible for orchestrating a series of brutal murders in 1969, including the Tate-LaBianca killings in Los Angeles. His manipulation and influence over his followers and the subsequent violent acts shocked the world and marked a dark chapter in American criminal history. Manson's actions and the Manson Family's crimes left a lasting impact on society.

## Bill Moyers (June 6th)

Bill Moyers is a respected American journalist, broadcaster, and public commentator. Throughout his career, he served in various roles, including as a news analyst, White House press secretary, and documentary producer. Moyers' contributions in journalism and broadcasting, particularly his commitment to investigative reporting and insightful commentary, earned him acclaim and respect within the field.

# Activity: "Profiles in Achievement: The Noteworthy Births of 1934"

Let's check your knowledge of the famous births of 1934. Choose the correct answer (a, b, c, d) for each question.

1. Born in 1934, who became a baseball legend famous for breaking Babe Ruth's home run record?
A) Giorgio Armani
B) Hank Aaron
C) Brian Epstein
D) Bill Moyers

2. Which fashion designer born in 1934 revolutionized the industry with elegant, minimalist designs?
A) Tom Baker
B) Roy Kinnear
C) Giorgio Armani
D) Brigitte Bardot

3. Who portrayed the fourth incarnation of the Doctor in the British series "Doctor Who" and was born in 1934?
A) Yuri Gagarinl
B) Roy Kinnear
C) Tom Baker
D) Brian Epstein

4. Who was born in 1934 and managed The Beatles to international fame?
A) Hank Aaron
B) Sophia Loren
C) Brian Epstein
D) Roy Kinnear

5. Which iconic actress born in 1934 became a symbol of beauty and talent in Hollywood?
A) Sophia Loren
B) Brigitte Bardot
C) Bill Moyers
D) Pat Boone

6. Which individual born in 1934 made history as the first human to journey into space?
A) Yuri Gagarin
B) Tom Baker
C) Giorgio Armani
D) Charles Manson

7. Born in 1934, who gained fame as a singer, actor, and TV personality known for his smooth voice?
A) Hank Aaron
B) Pat Boone
C) Roy Kinnear
D) Charles Manson

## We have heartfelt thank-you gifts for you

As a token of our appreciation for joining us on this historical journey through 1934, we've included a set of cards and stamps inspired by the year 1934. These cards are your canvas to capture the essence of the past. We encourage you to use them as inspiration for creating your unique cards and sharing your perspective on the historical moments we've explored in this book. Whether it's a holiday greeting or a simple hello to a loved one, these cards are your way to connect with the history we've uncovered together.

**Happy creating!**

# Activity Answers

**Chapter 1:**

1. A) The Night of the Long Knives
2. A) Adolf Hitler
3. C) U.S. Securities Exchange Act
4. C) The Revolution of 1934 in Spain
5. A) Ramsay MacDonald
6. B) Joseph Stalin
7. C) Franklin D. Roosevelt

**Chapter 2:**

1. B) Frank Capra
2. C) William Powell and Myrna Loy
3. C) Ancient Egypt
4. A) "Of Human Bondage"
5. C) Rothschild
6. B) Howard Hawks
7. C) "The Black Cat"

**Chapter 3:**

1. The Very Thought of You
2. Cocktails for Two
3. Love in Bloom
4. Winter Wonderland
5. You Ought to Be in Pictures

## Chapter 4:

| M | A | N | C | H | E | S | T | E | R | C | I | T | Y |
|---|---|---|---|---|---|---|---|---|---|---|---|---|---|
| N | T | H | E | L | E | N | J | A | C | O | B | S | A |
| A | R | N | A | S | T | O | I | V | O | N | E | N | I |
| G | E | I | H | O | R | T | O | N | S | M | I | T | H |
| I | L | J | H | A | R | S | E | N | A | L | A | O | I |
| T | L | S | A | T | R | F | Y | I | L | R | T | O | E |
| R | I | P | E | F | O | O | T | A | T | S | H | F | O |
| A | M | O | P | A | U | L | R | U | N | Y | A | N | H |
| H | N | R | S | G | P | H | D | R | N | D | A | A | T |
| N | E | T | N | N | R | N | P | L | E | C | L | L | E |
| A | D | O | I | H | I | J | R | E | R | E | M | L | N |
| O | L | M | A | L | Y | A | O | L | N | N | T | T | I |
| J | O | P | O | F | R | E | D | P | E | R | R | Y | E |
| O | G | H | C | A | R | L | H | U | B | B | E | L | L |

SPORT
ARNAS TOIVONEN
GOLDEN MILLER
OLIN DUTRA
FRED PERRY
MANCHESTER CITY
HORTON SMITH
ARSENAL
JOAN HARTIGAN
PAUL RUNYAN
HELEN JACOBS
CARL HUBBELL

## Chapter 6:
1. The Sikorsky S-42
2. 100
3. Scotland
4. England- Percy Shaw
5. George Nissen and Larry Griswold

## Chapter 8:

1. B) Hank Aaron
2. C) Giorgio Armani
3. C) Tom Baker
4. C) Brian Epstein
5. A) Sophia Loren
6. A) Yuri Gagarin
7. B) Pat Boone

# Embracing 1934: A Grateful Farewell

Embracing 1934: A Grateful Farewell

Thank you for joining us on this journey through a year that holds a special place in our hearts. Whether you experienced 1934 firsthand or through the pages of this book, we hope it brought you moments of joy, nostalgia, and connection to a time that will forever shine brightly in our memories.

Share Your Thoughts and Help Us Preserve History

Your support and enthusiasm for this journey mean the world to us. We invite you to share your thoughts, leave a review, and keep the spirit of '34 alive. As we conclude our adventure, we look forward to more journeys through the annals of history together. Until then, farewell and thank you for the memories.

We would like to invite you to explore more of our fantastic world by scanning the QR code below. There you can easily get free ebooks from us and receive so many surprises.

Copyright © Edward Art Lab 2023

All rights reserved. No part of this publication may be reproduced, distributed, or transmitted in any form or by any means, including photocopying, recording, or other electronic or mechanical methods, without the prior written permission of the publisher, except in the case of brief quotations embodied in critical reviews and certain other noncommercial uses permitted by copyright law.

# TO DO LIST

- ○ ---
- ○ ---
- ○ ---
- ○ ---
- ○ ---
- ○ ---
- ○ ---
- ○ ---
- ○ ---
- ○ ---
- ○ ---
- ○ ---
- ○ ---
- ○ ---

*well done!*

# To Do List

- [ ] _____
- [ ] _____
- [ ] _____
- [ ] _____
- [ ] _____
- [ ] _____
- [ ] _____
- [ ] _____
- [ ] _____
- [ ] _____
- [ ] _____
- [ ] _____
- [ ] _____
- [ ] _____

# TO DO LIST

Name: _____  Day: _____  Month: _____

| No | To Do List | Yes | No |
|----|------------|-----|----|
|    |            |     |    |
|    |            |     |    |
|    |            |     |    |
|    |            |     |    |
|    |            |     |    |
|    |            |     |    |
|    |            |     |    |
|    |            |     |    |
|    |            |     |    |
|    |            |     |    |
|    |            |     |    |
|    |            |     |    |
|    |            |     |    |

# TO DO LIST

Name: _____     Day: _____     Month: _____

| No | To Do List | Yes | No |
|----|------------|-----|-----|
|    |            |     |     |
|    |            |     |     |
|    |            |     |     |
|    |            |     |     |
|    |            |     |     |
|    |            |     |     |
|    |            |     |     |
|    |            |     |     |
|    |            |     |     |
|    |            |     |     |
|    |            |     |     |
|    |            |     |     |
|    |            |     |     |

# TO DO LIST

Name: _____  Day: _____  Month: _____

| No | To Do List | Yes | No |
|----|------------|-----|----|
|    |            |     |    |
|    |            |     |    |
|    |            |     |    |
|    |            |     |    |
|    |            |     |    |
|    |            |     |    |
|    |            |     |    |
|    |            |     |    |
|    |            |     |    |
|    |            |     |    |
|    |            |     |    |
|    |            |     |    |
|    |            |     |    |

# NOTE

# NOTE

Postcard
NE
NW
W
SW
S
SE

N
W
E
S
Greetings!
2
TIME TO
TRAVEL
PACIFIC OCEAN
MAP OF
THE WORLD

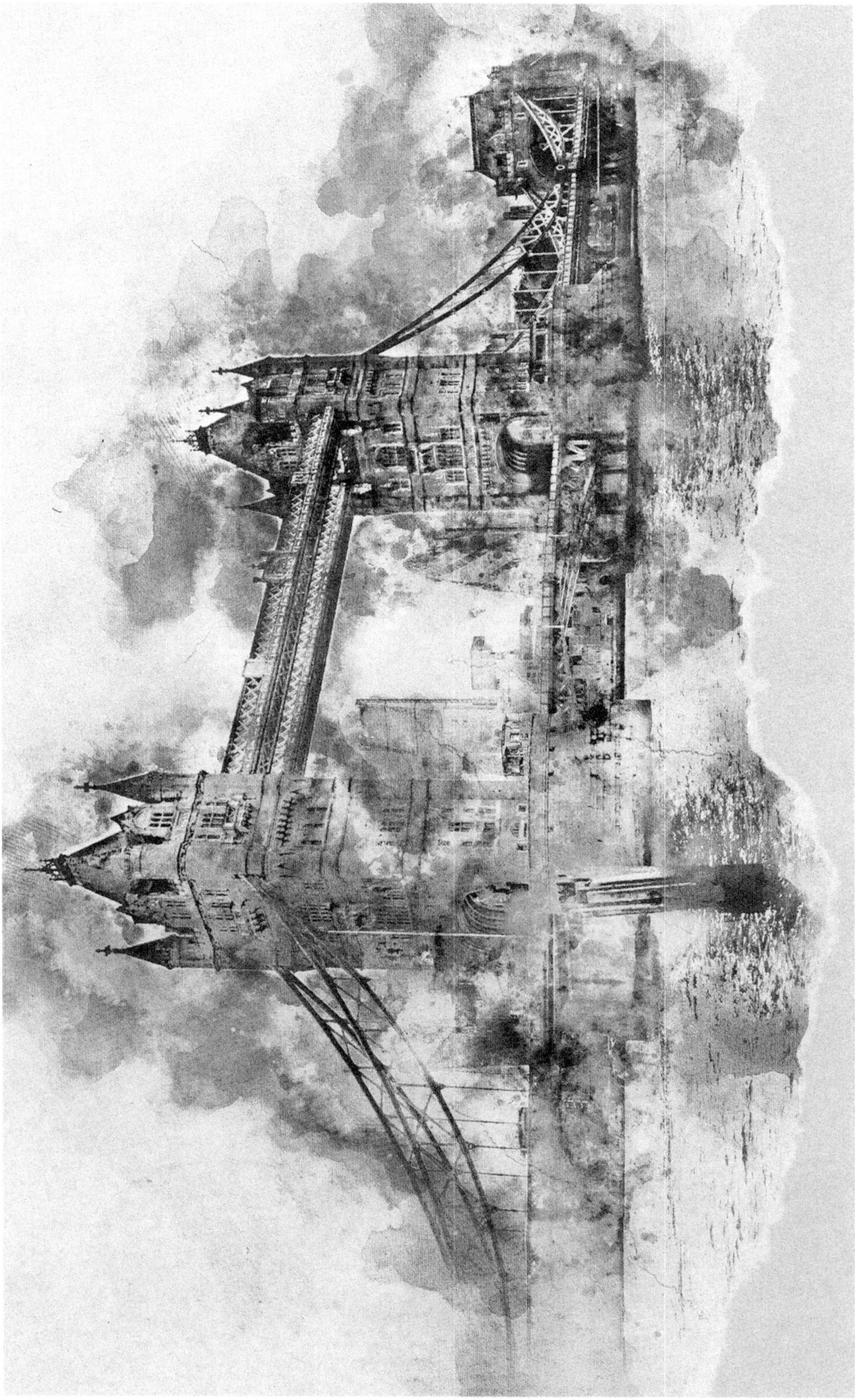

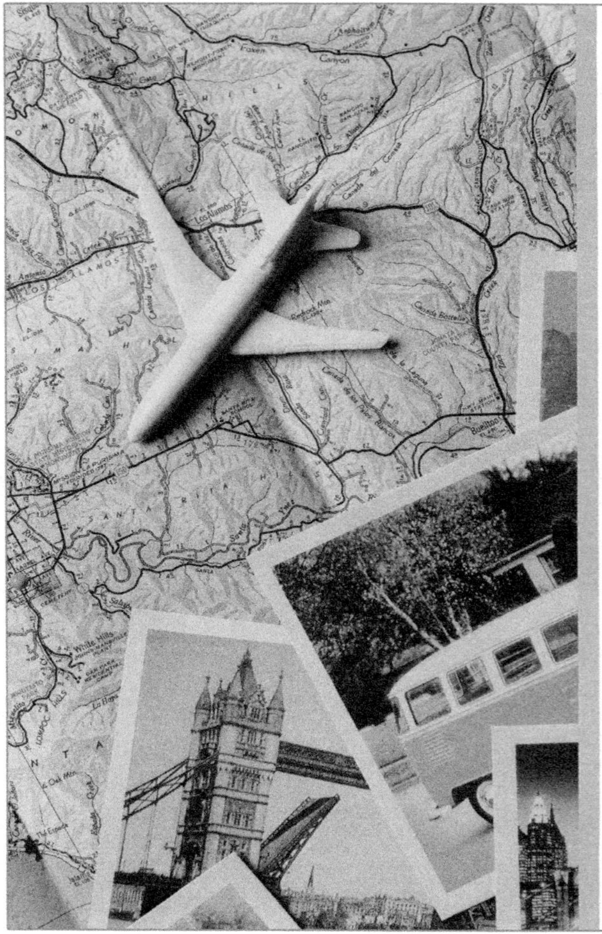

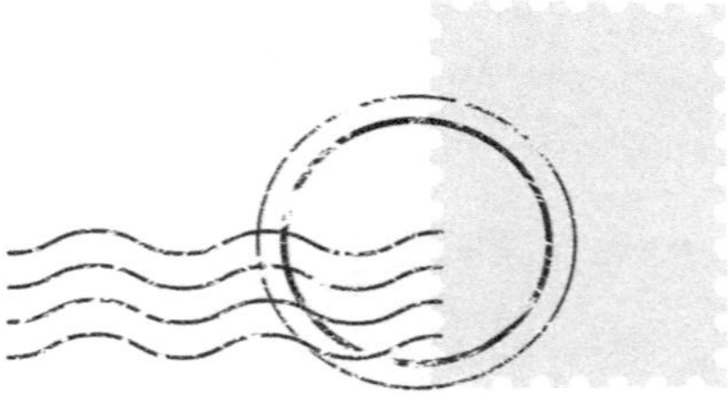

To:

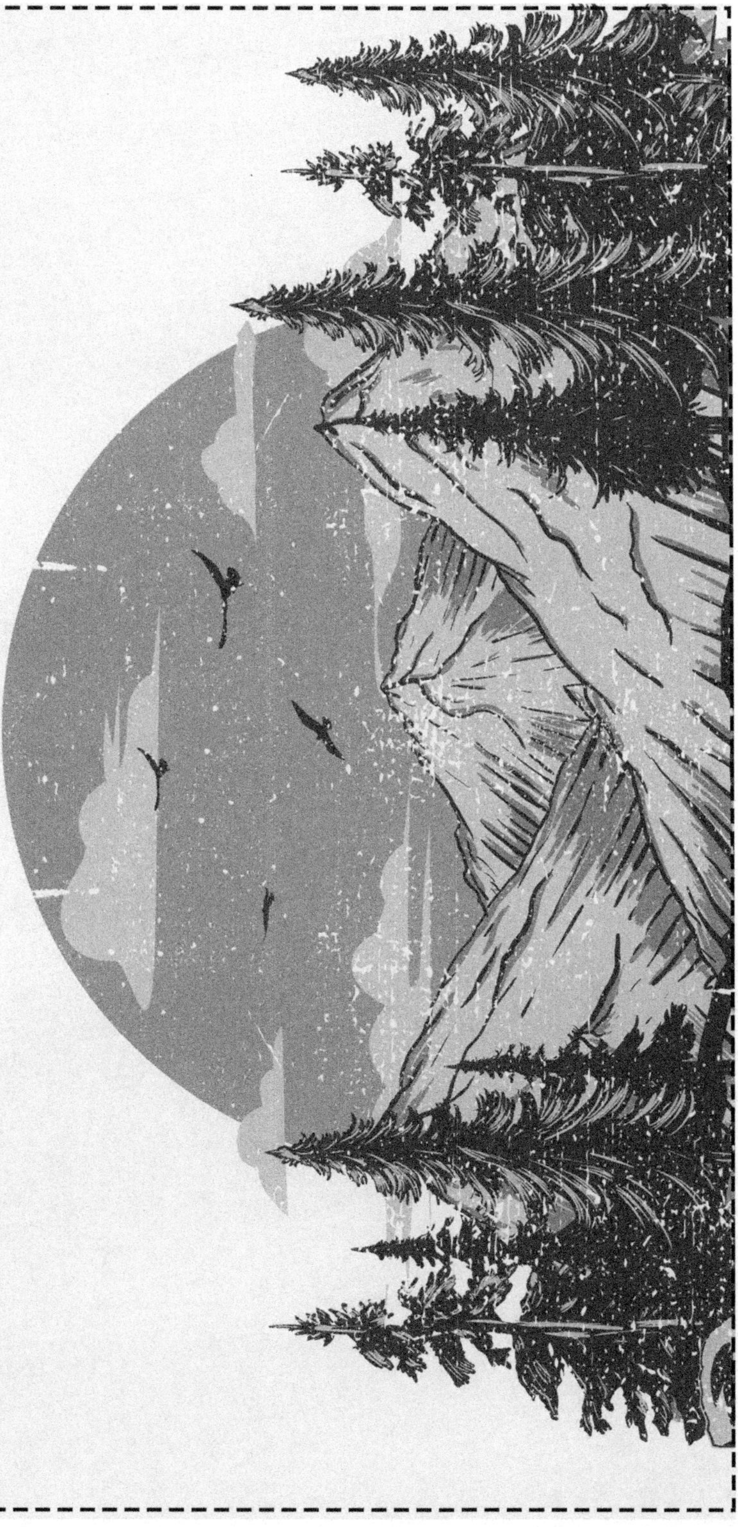

POSTCARD

To:

From:

*Remember This!*

WISH YOU WERE HERE,
123 ANYWHERE ST., ANY CITY

# TO DO List

# HAPPY BIRTHDAY NOTE

Printed in Great Britain
by Amazon